Back
from the

Brink

McDougal & Associates
Servants of Christ and Stewards of the
Mysteries of God

Back
from the
Brink

"The Enemy Tried To Take Me Out, but God Had Something Else In Mind"

By

Billy and Toni Webre

McDougal & Associates is dedicated to spreading the Gospel
of the Lord Jesus Christ to as many people as possible in the
shortest time possible.

Published by:

McDougal & Associates
18896 Greenwell Springs Road
Greenwell Springs, LA 70739
www,ThePublishedWord.com

ISBN: 978-1-950398-53-9

Printed on demand in the U.S., the U.K. and Australia
For Worldwide Distribution

Acknowledgements

As we went through the most difficult time of our life, we realize we didn't go through it alone. There were strangers who cared for me as if I was their own father:

- All the caregivers at Terrebonne General Hospital who took care of me, treating me with such respect and tenderness. That meant so much to me and my wife.

- Close friends who stuck by our side in our most difficult times. The fact that they were there through the ups and downs just proves to us that we could not have made it without them.

- We are so thankful for the prayer warriors who stood in the gap to bring about the miracles that brought me from death to full recovery. When the body of Christ unites for one purpose, nothing is impossible.

- We are also thankful for those who financially blessed us in a time that we were unable to work.

- Last, but certainly not least, we want to thank our Lord and Savior for providing healing for my body when the enemy wanted to take me out. Our only hope is that our lives will make a difference in the world around us because You didn't give up on us in the midst of our hopeless situation.

CONTENTS

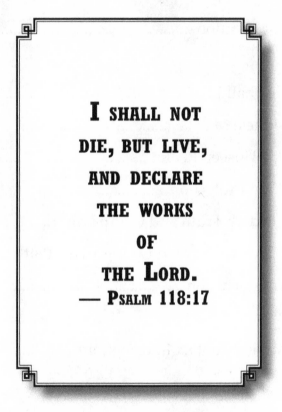

I SHALL NOT
DIE, BUT LIVE,
AND DECLARE
THE WORKS
OF
THE **L**ORD.
— **P**SALM 118:17

INTRODUCTION

Suddenly, I found myself on the edge of a spiritual battle, the brink, so to speak. Even though the experience I would soon face would change me and my wife for the better, it was not a pleasant place to be. I had no idea that day would end the way it did. I have found that being so close to the brink gives you greater perspective on life. It changes you. We will never be the same because of this battle.

Things in our new ministry were beginning to take shape. We could see God working on our behalf as never before. Our ministry began adopting an area in our community that was in tremendous need. Because of the connections we had in the community, people from multiple churches began working together with us to reach this neighborhood with food, prayer and the ministry of care to those who were desperate.

Just before my ordeal, I had been given a piece of property to use for our ministry there and was provided a building at another location to be used to train and raise up an army of soul-winners in our area. We had multiple churches, and over sixty people connected to our ministry, and it was growing.

I had received a word from the Lord eight years before to move from Cape Girardeau, Missouri, back to my hometown, Houma, Louisiana. As we began to prepare for the move, I went into a time of prayer and fasting.

As I was in prayer one day, the Lord gave me a word for my future in Louisiana. He said, "REACH Houma!" Then the Holy Spirit revealed to me what He meant by that.

R- Restore the Church back to the original

E- Evangelize the lost

A- Assemble the Body of Christ as a united force

C- Care for the needs of others

H- Healing for those who were spiritually and physically ill

As our ministry was taking off, it seemed that the enemy was not happy with what was going on. This book is an account of what happened to me and my wife in this spiritual battle. The enemy tried to take me out, but God had something else in mind.

Some portions in this book are my accounts, thoughts and experiences, while other parts are the account, thoughts and experiences of my wife, Toni. We learned so much through this battle that we knew we had to share it.

We would like to thank our children for being there for us in the most difficult time of our lives. You were a rock for your Mom and me, when it seemed all was lost. We would also like to thank our family for encouraging, praying and supporting us through it all. Also, to all of our friends: we are so thankful for you standing in the gap and believing that God was not finished with us yet. You have all been such a blessing to us in more ways than you can imagine.

As you read how God brought us through, open your heart to change. Let the Holy

Spirit activate you to be what God has called you to be in these last days. Please be mindful of those around you that need a miracle in their life. For some people, you are their only hope to experience Jesus on the earth today. If He did it for me, He can do it for you too.

Billy and Toni Webre
Gray, Louisiana

CHAPTER 1

HE SHALL LIVE AND NOT DIE

It was my birthday, and we decided to go to the beach and get in some much needed get-away time. It was to be a day trip with Toni chilling and me metal detecting. When we got home, I began to unload the car and noticed that my heart was in a weird rhythm. It would skip beats, then stop, then go slow. I'd had this happen before, but it would correct itself after a little while. This time, it didn't correct, so we decided to go to a local ER to get it checked out.

The ER doctor said my heart was in atrial fibrillation. They did a series of test and decided I would have a procedure done the next morning to shock my heart back into its normal rhythm. They kept me overnight to monitor me until the procedure could be done the next morning.

Thank You, Lord, that I stayed that night. At about 10 pm, I began having trouble breathing and started to panic. Toni began helping me, coaxing me on how to breathe—in through my nose and out through my mouth—so as not to hyperventilate. But it wasn't working. Nothing I did was working. Immediately nurses came in to give me something in my IV. That wasn't working either. Before long, I had passed out in Toni's arms.

(This is Toni's account of what happened. I don't remember anything else until I was in the CCU).

I was so scared and felt helpless. I watched my husband struggle just to breathe, and then he passed out in my arms. I didn't know what to do.

Suddenly, more than twenty people came into our room and began to work on Billy to save his life. One of the personnel tapped me on my shoulder softly and told me that I needed to leave the room. But something came over me. Boldness and steadfastness gripped me. I told him (without being rude), "I am not leaving. I will move out your way, but I'm staying."

As I positioned myself in the corner of the room by the door, I immediately began to pray. The Lord reminded me of a scripture, *"He shall live and not die to declare the works of the Lord."*

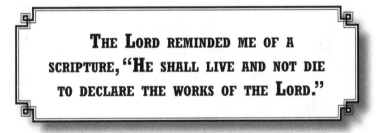

THE LORD REMINDED ME OF A SCRIPTURE, "HE SHALL LIVE AND NOT DIE TO DECLARE THE WORKS OF THE LORD."

MIRACLE #1

I couldn't believe what I was seeing. This team was like a well-oiled machine. Everyone had their place and knew just what to do. When one would get tired, another would take their place. It was definitely necessary, but for me, watching my husband in that condition was quite traumatizing. All I could do was pray.

Those caring professionals trying to revive my husband heard me praying, speaking in tongues, encouraging them not to give up. "Don't stop! Please don't stop!" All I could think is: this is not how it was supposed to be. God, You are not finished with Billy. *"He shall live and not die, and declare the works of the Lord."*

> "DON'T STOP! PLEASE DON'T STOP!" ALL I COULD THINK IS: THIS IS NOT HOW IT WAS SUPPOSED TO BE. GOD, YOU ARE NOT FINISHED WITH BILLY.

After quite a bit of time had passed, Billy finally took a deep breath. They checked for a pulse and found that his heart was beating a normal rhythm. This was MIRACLE #1.

They got Billy ready and rushed him out of the room to CCU. As I looked at his life-less body being wheeled by me, I noticed that he was a deep purple color. "He doesn't look alive," I said.

One of the nurses said to me, "He's going to be okay." It seemed that my constant prayers and the encouragement I was giving them gave them hope too. I felt like I had been doing serious warfare, but I knew the battle wasn't over.

After a few hours of waiting, I was told I could go see Billy in CCU, but then I would have to leave. I was not prepared for what I was about to see.

It was heartbreaking to see Billy hooked up to tubes and hoses, machines and IVs, and he was on a ventilator. Just a few hours before we had been talking and cutting up, thinking everything would be fine. Now this!

I remembered someone saying that people can hear what you are saying when they are lying there in this condition, so I whispered in Billy's ear, "Billy, I love you. You are going to be okay. I'll see you in the morning."

After leaving CCU that night, I sat in my car, overwhelmed by the events of the day.

All I could do was to weep uncontrollably. Then, after a while, I was able to regain control. I called my children and some close friends and told them what was going on. We needed all the prayer help we could get.

CHAPTER 2

MIRACLE MAN
(TONI'S STORY)

I was so tired, so emotionally on edge. I just had to get some rest. I tried my best to sleep, but sleep was just not happening. I knew I was in the fight of my life. It somehow felt like this battle would just be a precursor to battles to come.

The next morning a good friend came by to check on me, and while she was there (thank You, Lord), I had a phone call from Billy's doctor. He said to me, "Ma'am, your husband is the sickest person in our hospital right now. On a scale of 1 to 10, with 10 being the worst, your husband is a 9.5. All of his vital organs are shutting down. Also, he was without oxygen for more than ten minutes, and we think he most probably has damage to his brain and would be a vegetable if he survived.

The words he told me next would send my faith crashing, as it seemed that I had no hope: "You need to call your family. We only give Billy one or two days to live."

I would like to say that my faith grabbed me, and I became strong in that moment. But it didn't. I lost it! I really lost it!

How could faith and hope have sustained me through the events of these past two days, and then in an instant, it seemed, I could loose all the faith I had because of a few words spoken to me by a voice with an opposing view? It happened.

After many up and down moments that day, I had determined to believe the Word of the Lord. I also determined that everyone needed to be united in prayer. Everyone we called was told to pray Psalm 118:17 over my husband of almost forty-two years: *"He shall live and not die and declare the works of the Lord."*

When my children heard the news about their dad, they dropped everything and came from different parts of the country. They rallied together beautifully for me and for him. They all took on their part to encourage, get things in order and help to calm me down. They would say, "We are going to get through this, Momma!" And that meant the world to me.

There is nothing like the support of family and friends when your back is up against the wall, and you are faced with overwhelming odds against you. But there was another support being rallied at the same time. An army of prayer warriors was being organized that would bring about change in the heavenlies.

BUT THERE WAS ANOTHER SUPPORT BEING RALLIED AT THE SAME TIME. AN ARMY OF PRAYER WARRIORS WAS BEING ORGANIZED THAT WOULD BRING ABOUT CHANGE IN THE HEAVENLIES.

One of Billy's life missions had been to unite the churches in our community so that we could win the lost. This seemed to be part of the plan for his destiny. Now it was time for the community of believers to unite for him to receive his full healing, so that mission could be completed in the future. Wonderful friends and warriors organized a prayer meeting to be held outside the hospital where Billy was being treated. That evening, more than fifty people from a variety of churches gathered on their own free will with one goal—simply to pray for Billy.

There is something that happens in the heavenlies when the Body of Christ unites with one purpose. That is where the greatest anointing rests, and that is a recipe for a miracle.

I can truly say that my husband is alive and doing well today because of that prayer time, that was so precious to me and my family, and to God Himself. I later learned that there were people praying for Billy from Alaska to Africa. These were mighty prayer warriors who didn't give up on him. They recognized the call on his life, and they knew God was not finished with him. Their united declaration was: *"He shall live and not die and declare the works of the LORD."*

Prayer is not something that we only do as a last resort, but prayer does awaken Heaven to send help in time of need. And unified prayer sends legions of angels into the fray fighting for your cause. Unified prayer is noticed by Father God, and if God be for you, who can be against you.

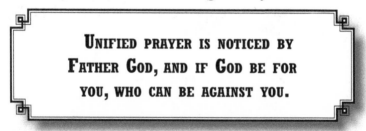

UNIFIED PRAYER IS NOTICED BY FATHER GOD, AND IF GOD BE FOR YOU, WHO CAN BE AGAINST YOU.

MIRACLE #2

Suddenly, Billy started doing better. Things started turning around. The doctors could not understand it and didn't have words to say to me at times.

As time progressed, they would recognize healing taking place and admit that it was indeed a miracle. As they shared their concerns for the future of Billy's health, those concerns were corrected by the healing virtue of the Lord Himself. What an awesome God! All negativity was being defeated by God's Word.

At my second visit to Billy in CCU, when I talked to him, he respond to me with his eyes blinking. I called the nurse in, and he responded to her commands by squeezing her hand. She said, "He's not brain dead! Look how he's responding. This was MIRACLE #2.

MIRACLE #3

While the prayer warriors were still gathered outside the hospital, I came out the front doors and was met with the sight of these beautiful people, gathered together, praying for Billy. My heart was so filled with overwhelming love for them that I just had to go and hug each of them.

I shared with them one of the doctors' concerns, that Billy's kidneys were still not working, and so he would have to be transferred to a hospital with a dialysis machine. One of the pastors who was there started to immediately pray that Billy's kidneys would produce bags and bags of urine. That struck everyone there as funny, and they all laughed. But, at my next visit to Billy in CCU, the nurses told me they could barely keep up with the amount of urine being produced by Billy's kidneys. Praise God! That was MIRACLE #3.

MIRACLE # 4

At one point, there were concerns about Billy's heart not pumping enough blood to supply his body. The staff asked for permission to insert a device that would help the heart beat, to give it relief. They took Billy to the cath lab to do this procedure.

Before the procedure, they checked blood flow once more. While they had Billy on the table, monitoring the blood flow, his blood began to circulate throughout his body. There was no longer a need to put in the device to help his heart. This was MIRACLE

#4. All the doctors could say was, "Billy is a Miracle Man!" Of course, we knew who the real Miracle Worker was.

> **ALL THE DOCTORS COULD SAY WAS, "BILLY IS A MIRACLE MAN!" OF COURSE, WE KNEW WHO THE REAL MIRACLE WORKER WAS.**

MIRACLE #5

Because Billy was beginning to turn around for the good, the doctors decided to began weaning him off of the sedation that he was on and getting him ready to take out the breathing and feeding tubes that had kept him alive for the past two days. He was more aware of his surroundings and would write notes on a paper to let us know what he needed. He was doing very well and being very cooperative with the nurses.

Then, while nurses were cleaning him up one day, he asked to be untied, to get some relief for his hands. But when they untied him, Billy quickly grabbed the tubes that were in his mouth and pulled them out. Everyone was shocked and didn't know if they would have to put the tubes back in or not. They waited to see what would happen, and as they waited, they noticed that Billy's vitals were acceptable, so they decided to leave the tubes out. This was MIRACLE #5.

MIRACLE #6

When the doctors told me about what had happened, they said that Billy would not be able to talk, let alone sing, ever again, because of the way the tubes had been pulled out. On my next visit, Billy was talking to me in a whisper, but I knew God was at work. Billy needed his voice to "declare the works of the Lord." Today he is talking and singing as if it all had never happened. This was MIRACLE #6.

> **BILLY NEEDED HIS VOICE TO "DECLARE THE WORKS OF THE LORD." TODAY HE IS TALKING AND SINGING AS IF IT ALL HAD NEVER HAPPENED.**

MIRACLE #7

Billy's recovery in CCU was much quicker than the doctors or nurses ever thought it could be. Within five days of being in CCU, his doctor informed me that they were transferring him to a normal room. Usually, the doctor said, a patient would have been expected to be in CCU for a week, in ICU a week, in a regular room a week, and then in a physical therapy facility for a month. Billy stayed in the regular room for just five days and then was released to go home under my care. He was well enough to skip ICU and in-house physical therapy. This was MIRACLE #7.

I learned, through this experience, that Faith comes by hearing and hearing by the

Word of God. When God speaks His Word to us, He is giving us the authority to command that Word. Faith is activated by how we act upon the Word God has given to us.

> **GOD IS GIVING US THE AUTHORITY TO COMMAND THAT WORD. FAITH IS ACTIVATED BY HOW WE ACT UPON THE WORD GOD HAS GIVEN TO US.**

I have also learned, through this experience, that God is still in the miracle-working business. This will bring much hope to many people in the days ahead. God is so faithful. When we are faced with impossibilities, we can trust Him. What an awesome God we serve. Billy is truly a Miracle Man, but it is only because of God's faithfulness!

CHAPTER 3

THE UNSEEN REALM
(BILLY)

When I regained consciousness in the CCU, while hope had come back to my body and things were getting better, I found myself facing a different kind of fight. I was on the brink of a spiritual battle that has defined who I am today. While my body was in a state of miraculous healing, I was fighting a battle in the unseen realm and found myself in desperation for relief.

The real world was unacceptable to me at the time. What I was seeing, feeling, smelling and experiencing was so much of a shock to my senses that I was desperately trying to escape it.

I had never felt like I had to escape my reality in this way before. And I had never been so desperate for things to change. I would close my eyes, to try to sleep, to try to make the time go faster, allowing my body to rest. I was so tired and wanted desperately to sleep, but I couldn't.

Every time I would close my eyes, I would see (as I know it to be today) a different dimension of the unseen world that was around me. Seeing, hearing and feeling this was very troubling to me. I had never experienced anything like this in my entire life. It was as if I was witnessing what was going on in the spiritual realm around me. It was dark and disturbing, and it affected my senses.

What I was seeing and hearing would disturb me so much that it made me open my eyes, only bringing me back to a reality that was unacceptable to me. This reality was not a good place to be. I was so uncomfortable in the real world—the pain, the nausea, being stuck in a bed and stripped of all dignity. I was longing for the touch and tenderness of my wife, but I had been informed that she could only visit me twice a day for one hour at a time. It seemed that it took forever for those times to come. The clock seemed to drag by, as I waited for those visiting hours.

I would close my eyes, just to try to escape this reality. But every time my eyes would close to try get some much-needed sleep, I would see what was going on around me in another dimension. I would see and feel the evil that was surrounding me. Evil spirits were trying to bring me to the brink of despair and hopelessness. This was very disturbing.

I could hear what was being said. I could see creatures that were deformed, plotting against me, trying to pull me into their world of hopelessness. I would desperately cry out to God for understanding.

When I couldn't take it anymore I would open my eyes, only to be awakened to the reality of the real world and my situation. The clock represented my reality, but it moved so terribly slow.

Then the nausea would flood me again and the pain I was in because of the violent ordeal of more than twenty people having worked on me to bring me back to life through chest compressions and electric shock just a few days before. Every time I would cough, the pain would be excruciating, and I would cough up blood—the result of me pulling the breathing and feeding tubes out just days before.

Needless to say, I found no rest ... until my wife would come with such hope and encouragement. The nurses who watched my vitals said that I did so much better when she was there with me. It was as if Jesus Himself had entered the room.

One time, when she was there, I fell into a deep and peaceful sleep, as she gently sang a song of worship to God in my ear:

You are great;
You do miracles so great,
There is no one else like You.
There is no one else like You.[1]

Even as I was on the brink of spiritual warfare, in the midst of the battle of my

---

life, such a peace flooded my soul in that moment. While Toni was there, I had relief from the battle.

It is so important for family members, loved ones and friends of those who are fighting for others not to give up, not to give in to the fears of what they see or what the doctors may say in a bad report. When the doctors would give another bleak prognosis, Toni would say, "No, I don't believe that. Billy will live and not die and declare the works of the Lord."

I know of a certainty today, that if my wife, my family, my friends and others who were praying for me had given up, I would not be here today. Don't grow weary in well doing, for in good season you will reap if you faint not (see Galatians 6:9).

The battle I was in did not end until I left CCU to go into a regular room. I found it so odd that the minute I was moved into room 316 (isn't that just like God—John 3:16) the warfare stopped. I was at peace and could sense the presence of God.

It was amazing. I could actually see waves of His glory in my room. When I closed my eyes, I saw gold colored sparkles illuminating my eyes. What a contrast to what I had been seeing and feeling in CCU!

That first night, I still had a hard time sleeping because of the experience of the past few days. The battle was definitely real, but I didn't understand why I'd had to go through those things in CCU.

That night, the Holy Spirit began to reveal to me what God had been doing in me and through me in this battle, and I began to write on my phone the thoughts God was giving me about it all. (Remember, they told Toni I would have brain damage. It is a miracle that I was able to form thoughts and write them down.) The Holy Spirit filled my room, and I couldn't hold back the tears as I wrote.

Toni and I would stay up late into the night talking about my experiences and hers, what God had done and what He had said. We were determined to do it all together in the future.

What a miracle working God we serve! And what good friends we have! My family was such a blessing, especially to Toni in the midst of the battle that brought me back from the brink. I am forever grateful for all that God has done for us. I knew that what we went through would bring great hope to many people in the future, and the story had to be told. I was alive to declare the goodness of God!

CHAPTER 4

WHAT PROTECTION!

(This is what the Lord showed me and I wrote in my phone that first night in my room as the Holy Spirit flooded my heart with understanding and His awesome presence.)

All my life I have been blessed to live with protection from the world of evil and desperation. I have never felt threatened or hopeless to the point of despair, as I have seen in so many people I have met on the streets as an evangelist.

Over the course of my life, as a Christ follower and soul-winner, I have met many people and couldn't understand why they didn't just surrender to this saving Jesus. Why was it such a struggle for them to let

go of the despair and heartache and to receive peace, forgiveness and hope? This is
why I was allowed to experience what they
experience, to be touched with a heart of
compassion and empathy and know what
they are going through.

How can I have true compassion and
empathy without going through the desperation many do every single day? Going
through this experience has truly opened
my eyes to a world that is not seen, to the
point that fear gripped me to the core. I was
on the brink, with the reality of where I was,
what I was experiencing in my body, and
the need for escape that only led to more
hopelessness and despair.

As I opened my eyes I would fix them
on the clock placed directly above me. That
clock was the reality of where I was at the
moment. How slow that clock would move!
And how I needed to close my eyes just to
escape this reality!

I knew that my wife would be there twice
a day for an hour, and how that hour would
bring me hope! Oh, such peace would flood

my heart when she walked in the door. "There's my miracle man," she would say. "God is doing things that only He can do!"

In my limited reality, all I could see was the tubes, all I could feel was the excruciating pain, and all I could smell were smells that violated all my senses and brought me to the point of nausea.

But that reality was erased when Toni walked into that room. It was as if Jesus Himself had walked in, with all His authority and splendor. My lovely wife took control of my environment as if she owned it.

Isn't that what God has been doing for me all my protected life? He placed His angels to have charge over me. He shielded me from the harm of the unseen world of evil. But I have been naive and selfish to think that everyone has had the same experience of protection as me. Many are trapped, destitute, and hopeless, completely void of this protection. This is not because Jesus doesn't care, but because most people haven't realized how much He really loves them.

Even though Jesus paid such a great price for this hope, many can't see the lifeline that is right in front of them.

> **EVEN THOUGH JESUS PAID SUCH A GREAT PRICE FOR THIS HOPE, MANY CAN'T SEE THE LIFELINE THAT IS RIGHT IN FRONT OF THEM.**

The lost are lost because they are trapped with the reality of where they are in this natural world, and the fact that it is not an acceptable place to be. In their need to escape their reality, they find temporary relief through alcohol and drugs or whatever helps them escape. But this remedy leaves them in the darkness of this demonically-controlled life.

This experience allowed me to be put in a place where it seemed hopeless, so that I could know what others are feeling. If I can only be more effective in seeing where people are, I can help them get to their Savior. That is my heart's true desire.

I have preached the truth to the lost, showed them the way, pleaded with them, prayed for them, only to find them all too often going back to the lifestyle that holds them captive. There must be a way to get through to them! How can I be more effective in helping others see Jesus for who He really is?

CHAPTER 5

NEEDED: TRUTH AND COMPASSION

When I got to my regular hospital room, I began to recover very quickly. This continued to amaze everyone, especially the doctors and nurses. We had a flow of healthcare workers coming into our room on a regular basis: taking vitals, giving me breathing treatments and physical therapy, delivering food and drink, etc. It seemed to be non-stop.

These were not conditions conducive to sleep, so Toni and I talked about everything. She would tell me about how our kids were helping her, how other people encouraged her so much, and all the things God did for

47

us in the midst of this battle. I would tell her what I had been going through while in CCU, what God was speaking to me, and how blessed we were. I am so thankful that I had someone there for me.

One night, around 2 am, we were still talking when a respiratory therapist came into my room to give me another breathing treatment. When she walked in, she was shocked and awed to see that it was me. As it turned out, she had been one of the team members of the "code blue" team that had revived me a few days earlier. She couldn't believe that I was sitting up and doing so well. Immediately I began to feel the presence of the Holy Spirit come into our room.

At first, we just listened to her. Then the Lord began to give me questions to ask her about herself, her family and how she was doing with all the Covid patients she was dealing with. Toni is so gifted at this, but something had changed in me. I felt compassion for what this woman was going through, and it touch me to the core of my soul. The Lord was allowing me to experience what she was experiencing.

I felt that I needed to pray for her, so I asked her, "Can we pray for you?" She agreed. As I touched her hand, to hold it and pray, I felt the presence of the Lord go straight through me. I have felt that before, but never in that capacity. I could feel God's love pour into her, and she felt it too.

Immediately she began to weep. What an amazing experience! Jesus' compassion invaded this vessel that had been emptied by the truth of what she was going through. We allowed her to open up her heart with the truth of where she was, and God showed compassion on her through us, His vessels.

Toni has the ministry of hugs, and she asked the lady, "Can I hug you"?

She grabbed Toni and cried, sobbing, as a release came to her. In the process, she let go of all the fear and all the doubt. Jesus came into my room that night, and He brought such a healing to her.

It seemed that God was giving us many opportunities to minister while we were there in my hospital room, to the point that it seemed as if people were just waiting outside the door of our room, listening in and coming in with the hope that we would pray for them. God would give us prophetic words to speak over some. We were able to pray for their safety, their families, their futures. It was amazing what God was doing!

> *But instead we will remain strong and always sincere in our love as we express the truth. All our direction and ministries will flow from Christ and lead us deeper into him, the anointed Head of his body, the church. For his "body" has been formed in his image and is closely joined together and constantly connected as one. And every member has been given divine gifts to contribute to the growth of all; and as these gifts operate effectively throughout the whole body, we are built up and made perfect in love.*
> Ephesians 4:15-16, TPT

TRUTH

Because the enemy is a liar and the father of lies, truth is always being attacked in the world today. We can see clearly that lies are the enemy's weapon of choice right now. Those who are bound by sin and addictions have, ultimately, been lied to. The thing is: they believed these lies the enemy has told them, and the lie they believe is what holds them in their prison.

The one bound by greed believes the lie that if they can only get more, then they will be happy. The one who is bound by heroin lives for their next fix. The one who lives to party believes that this is the only way to have joy in life. These lies are embedded in there thoughts because the reality of where they are drives them to find a way to escape their reality, and their soul is turned into a stronghold based upon these lies.

Eventually, everything they do is done to make their lie become their truth. Of course, it can never become truth, because it's all a lie.

Lies have no control over those that don't believe them. When we encounter people who are being controlled by lies, we must know what they believe and how they came to believe it. This may take some time to discover, so we have to be good listeners, to truly find out where people are.

This can also be revealed to us through the unction of the gifts of the Spirit. Then, lies that are confronted with Truth become a battleground. There will be a fight.

Jesus was crucified because He spoke the truth of God's Kingdom wherever He went, and two things happened:

1. Those who had a vested interest in the lies they believed (the religious leaders) were in opposition to Jesus' truths.
2. Those who received the truth, who were of a humble spirit and were open to it, were set free.

The Truth either makes you free, or it makes you mad. This is the indicator of who we are to target in these last days. The truth spoken reveals the condition of the heart. You can tell when a person is humble or

> **THE TRUTH EITHER MAKES YOU FREE OR IT MAKES YOU MAD. THIS IS THE INDICATOR OF WHO WE ARE TO TARGET IN THESE LAST DAYS.**

hell bent on believing the lies they currently believe.

I believe there is a way around these lies. It is the gifts of the Spirit in operation in the lives of the believer who can reveal the true heart of those we are ministering to. If you are interested in learning more, please read 1 Corinthians 12:4-11. All the gifts of the Spirit are to be used to demonstrate God's love for humanity.

> **ALL THE GIFTS OF THE SPIRIT ARE TO BE USED TO DEMONSTRATE GOD'S LOVE FOR HUMANITY.**

For example:

- A word of knowledge given to us by the Spirit reveals things about people to us that only God knows, and this opens their hearts to Him.

- A prophetic word given to us by the Spirit reveals the heart of God about that person, and this gives them worth.
- The gift of healing brings physical and spiritual healing to a person, and this reveals God's love and care for them.

The gifts of the Spirit are given as the Spirit leads for what is needed in each and every situation.

COMPASSION

Compassion: "to have the bowels, yearn, to feel sympathy or empathy toward others."

Truth without compassion hardens the heart of those who believe the lies, so they cannot be affected by the truth. If we give God's truth without compassion, it causes an unbeliever to reject that truth.

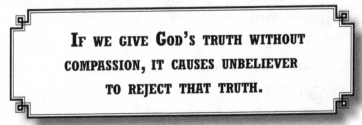

IF WE GIVE GOD'S TRUTH WITHOUT COMPASSION, IT CAUSES UNBELIEVER TO REJECT THAT TRUTH.

It was Jesus' compassion for the hurting, the sick and the demon possessed that moved Him to do miracles for them. This compassion was heartfelt. It was Jesus being touched by the feeling of their infirmities. He was *"moved with tender compassion"* (Mark 1:41, TPT).

Many want to see miracles, so they can be well known or to prove their ministry to be legit. But the motives of the heart is everything when it comes to God moving in miracles.

God was changing hearts that day without me or Toni praying a prayer for the people we met for salvation. It was real to the core.

The Lord spoke to me that night, when I could finally gather all my thoughts on this and said, "This is what I want to do with the last-days army." He wants truth and compassion working in the lives of every believer to affect the world around us.

> **GOD WANTS TRUTH AND COMPASSION WORKING IN THE LIVES OF EVERY BELIEVER TO AFFECT THE WORLD AROUND US.**

And every member has been given divine gifts to contribute to the growth of all; and as these gifts operate effectively throughout the whole body, we are built up and made perfect in love. Ephesians 4:16, TPT

The time is coming when every Christ lover who hears His voice will be used in the gifts that God has given them. They will be effective in reaching the lost because their motivation will be truth and compassion for those whom the Holy Spirit sends their way. No longer can the Church be dependant upon one person to flow in the gifts. There will be opportunity for all to be used by God.

Truth without compassion makes the unbeliever harder and closed off to a relationship with Jesus, leaving the unbeliever not knowing the true nature of God.

Compassion without truth may feed and care for them, but it enables the unbeliever to stay in the state of hopelessness and despair because their reality will never change without truth.

Truth and compassion introduce a loving God to a sin-sick world. The greatest hope for the unbeliever is that God can change them through relationship. It's all about relationship. The Father adopts us, calling us His own. It's the truth that makes us free, but it's His love that keeps us free.

About a month before this ordeal at the hospital, the Lord allowed me to see in the Spirit a portal that opened up in the heavenlies. I saw Jesus standing in the midst of a great host of mighty angels. It was as if He was giving instruction to the angels. There was an excitement in the air, an expectancy, as the Lord pointed to the angels and gave them their assignments. Then, all of a sudden, I heard the Lord say with a loud voice, "It's harvest time!"

It is time for the last-days Church to be more effective than it's ever been. Jesus is sending the angelic help that we need. We must engage, find our place, and reach out to those who have not yet experienced the gift of salvation.

CHAPTER 6

WHAT WE LEARNED THROUGH THIS BATTLE

We learned many things through this experience. Here are some of them:

WE LEARNED TO ASK GOD WHAT HE SAYS ABOUT A SITUATION

When Toni was alone, frightened and not knowing what to do, faced with the battle of her life, she asked God, "How do I pray Lord?" Psalms 118:17 was what the Lord gave her to declare and decree. *"He shall live and not die, and declare the works of the LORD."* It was the Word of God that demanded a response. God hears His Word when those in authority take it by faith and declare it over a situation.

> GOD HEARS HIS WORD WHEN THOSE IN AUTHORITY TAKE IT BY FAITH AND DECLARE IT OVER A SITUATION.

Many have asked me if I had a Heaven encounter when I died for more than an hour. All I can tell them is this: No, the last thing I remember was not being able to breath and passing out in my wife's arms. The next thing I remember was when I was in CCU right after I pulled out the tubes.

Since then, I asked the Lord, "Why didn't I see You or Heaven when I died?"

The Lord showed me that when Toni spoke God's Word over me with authority, the angel that carries our spirit to the heavenly portal had to obey God's Word: HE SHALL LIVE AND NOT DIE. I was on hold till God said it was time to live. Those words spoken in faith and desperation was what brought my body back to life, when God said it was time.

God's Word declares:

> *So then, faith comes by hearing and hearing by the word of God.*
>
> Romans 10:17, NKJV

When God speaks a word to you, it is your response to that word that activates faith in your situation. Faith is our reaction to what we know God is saying to us.

> **WHEN GOD SPEAKS A WORD TO YOU, IT IS YOUR RESPONSE TO THAT WORD THAT ACTIVATES FAITH IN YOUR SITUATION. FAITH IS OUR REACTION TO WHAT WE KNOW GOD IS SAYING TO US.**

(TONI)

When God gives you a word, you must hold tight to that word and never let it go. Never give up on it. Never doubt that God has said it, and that He can and will perform it.

When the doctors said Billy would not live, God said, "He will." Which one should I believe? That is why every time I was given a bad report, I would respond, "I don't believe that!" I kept believing and speaking God's Word on every subject. Faith is when you know that you know. Then you can trust that it will come to past. We cannot, and we must not give up on what God has said to us.

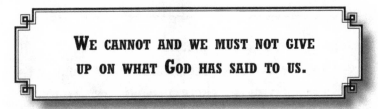

WE CANNOT AND WE MUST NOT GIVE UP ON WHAT GOD HAS SAID TO US.

(BILLY)

Noah was told by God to build an ark, so that his family would be saved. Noah obeyed God (by faith), and one hundred years later, he was still building the ark. Now that is persistent faith! I asked the Lord one day about Noah, and He said to me that

He did not have to tell Noah twice to build the Ark. Standing, trusting, believing and holding fast to what God has spoken ... that is faith!

WE LEARNED THAT IT'S IMPORTANT TO HAVE FRIENDS

It was our friends, the ones we had poured into, ministered to, connected with, encouraged, spent our time with, mentored, cried with and prayed for who stood by our side in our worst possible moment. They were the ones who poured back into us when our vessels were empty. Though this, we learned that the work and love that we pour into our friends is worth it all.

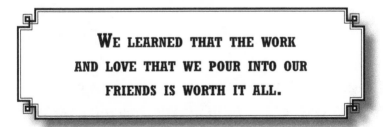

WE LEARNED THAT THE WORK AND LOVE THAT WE POUR INTO OUR FRIENDS IS WORTH IT ALL.

So many believers want to isolate themselves from others. They are fearful that they will be hurt if they get too close to those they minister to. Yes, we have been hurt by people we got close to, but the positive always outweighs the negative, when it comes to relationships. We have learned that forgiveness is better than bitterness, that closeness is better that isolation.

The Bible relates this interesting story:

> *A certain woman of the wives of the sons of the prophets cried out to Elisha, saying, "Your servant my husband is dead, and you know that your servant feared the LORD. And the creditor is coming to take my two sons to be his slaves."*
>
> *So Elisha said to her, "What shall I do for you? Tell me, what do you have in the house?"*
>
> *And she said, "Your maidservant has nothing in the house but a jar of oil."*
>
> *Then he said, "Go, borrow vessels from everywhere, from all your neighbors— empty vessels; do not gather just a few. And when you have come in, you shall shut the door behind you and your sons;*

then pour it into all those vessels, and set aside the full ones."

So she went from him and shut the door behind her and her sons, who brought the vessels to her; and she poured it out. Now it came to pass, when the vessels were full, that she said to her son, "Bring me another vessel."

And he said to her, "There is not another vessel." So the oil ceased.

2 Kings 4:1-6, NKJV

The amount of oil this women received as a miracle was in direct proportion to the amount of friends she had.

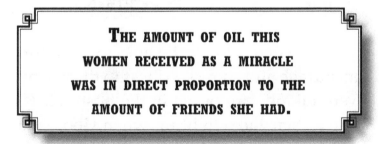

THE AMOUNT OF OIL THIS WOMEN RECEIVED AS A MIRACLE WAS IN DIRECT PROPORTION TO THE AMOUNT OF FRIENDS SHE HAD.

Making friends and connections with the heart of love, care and concern for others provides you a network of people who will fight for you when it is needed the most. Our miracle was connected with our friends. They were the army that stood in the gap when we needed them.

WE LEARNED THAT WE CAN STILL MINISTER TO OTHERS WHILE IN THE BATTLE

But sanctify the Lord God in your hearts, and always be ready to give a defense to everyone who asks you a reason for the hope that is in you, with meekness and fear. 1 Peter 3:15, NKJV

It was such a joy to be able to pray for, encourage and show kindness to those who were taking care of me in the hospital. To watch their faces light up when God gave us prophetic word to them to speak life to their situation was an awesome experience.

At the time I was in the hospital, the Covid-19 virus was attacking many people in our community. As a consequence, the large hospital I was in was completely full. This weighed heavily on every caregiver there. They were stressed, worried, fearful for themselves and their families. The long hours were also taking a toll on them. Toni and I noticed immediately and prayed for the Lord to give us wisdom concerning how to minister to them.

As they came into the room, God would began to show us things about what they were facing. We would tell them that they were so caring and that we were so thankful for them. The Lord would give us questions to ask them like. " How are you dealing with all that is going on?" They were shocked that we cared. The amount of people we were able to minister to was amazing.

One of my physical therapists was walking with me down the hall for exercise, and she told me, "You seem to be positive with all of what you are going through."

I said, "Oh, I could be negative, but I choose to stay positive."

When she was leaving I told her to have a great day. She said, "I am choosing to be positive today."

When we are being tested, we tend to focus on ourselves and what we are going through. But every test can be a testimony ... if we let it be. There are people all around us who need Jesus. This world is so cruel. When the Body of Christ lives like Jesus, the world recognizes Him in us. This is the greatest witnessing tool of all.

WE LEARNED THAT THERE IS POWER IN UNITY

Behold, how good and how pleasant it is for brethren to dwell together in unity! It is like the precious oil upon the head, running down on the beard, the beard of Aaron, running down on the edge of his garments. It is like the dew of Hermon, descending upon the mountains of Zion; for there the LORD commanded the blessing—life forevermore.

Psalm 133:1-3, NKJV

Those who have completely surrendered to the Lord and have their names written in the Book of Life will one day be united together in Heaven. We will be worshiping as one voice and one Body. There will be no denominations in Heaven. All differences in doctrine will fade away. We will know completely what it is like to be unified. Oh, what a day that will be!

More then fifty people from multiple denominations and churches came to the hospital parking lot that evening to pray for me. When believers from Alaska to Africa unified in prayer for me to live and not die, Heaven took notice.

The anointing for healing came to me because compassion led believers to gather for my sake, for one cause, for *my* cause. I am here today, doing what God has called me to do, because of the Body of Christ coming together in unity.

We must put aside our differences, our petty disagreements, our hurts from the past, and unite and work together for the sake of the lost in our communities. What if the Body of Christ from every denomination and church would unite to win the lost? Heaven would take notice. We would see the greatest awakening ever known to man.

WE LEARNED THAT TRUTH AND COMPASSION CHANGE THE HEART OF THE UNBELIEVER

TRUTH

Every person lives in their own reality. I can't understand what they are going through or what lies they believe, unless I listen to them. So, first, before anything else,

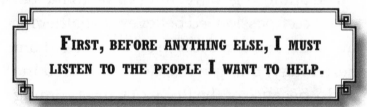

FIRST, BEFORE ANYTHING ELSE, I MUST LISTEN TO THE PEOPLE I WANT TO HELP.

I must listen to them.

And it takes time to listen. I have to focus on them and what they are saying, without being distracted. As I listen to them, I can start to understand their delusions and false beliefs. They have been lied to, and they believe the lie.

These lies are what hold them captive. This is their truth, what they believe to be truth. If I don't know the lies they believe, how can I present the truth of God's Word to those lies? God's Word is the real truth, and it is the truth that makes us free.

Attached to all the lies of the enemy there is a network of demonic strongholds that holds people captive, keeping them bound up. For instance:

- **The addicted** — The pain they suffer from detox when they're not using drugs holds them to the lie that they can't be free
- **The abused**—The fear of loosing financial support if they break away from the abuser keeps them going back for more abuse.
- **The unbeliever**—They think that if they believe there is no God, then there is no consequences for their sin, which strengthens their delusion.

- **The religious**—They think that their good works will get them to Heaven, so they don't call on God with repentance. They don't think they need to.

These are examples of the network of lies the enemy places in the minds of those that God wants to be free. When we truly care to spend time and listen to those that God puts into our path, we exhibit the heart of the Lord Himself.

> **WHEN WE TRULY CARE TO SPEND TIME AND LISTEN TO THOSE THAT GOD PUTS INTO OUR PATH, WE EXHIBIT THE HEART OF THE LORD HIMSELF.**

We must be willing to do whatever is necessary to build up enough trust with them, going back and loving them again and again until a relationship is formed. In this way, we can demonstrate God's love with truth. People won't know how much we care, until we care enough to get to know them.

> **PEOPLE WON'T KNOW HOW MUCH WE CARE, UNTIL WE CARE ENOUGH TO GET TO KNOW THEM.**

Second, I must listen to the Holy Spirit. There are things that we could never know about people that we encounter in our ministry outreach. That is why it is so important to allow the Holy Spirit to speak to us and see what He says about them.

> **THERE ARE THINGS THAT WE COULD NEVER KNOW ABOUT PEOPLE THAT WE ENCOUNTER IN OUR MINISTRY OUTREACH. THAT IS WHY IT IS SO IMPORTANT TO ALLOW THE HOLY SPIRIT TO SPEAK TO US AND SEE WHAT HE SAYS ABOUT THEM.**

One word from the Lord to a troubled soul can change everything in a instant.

> **ONE WORD FROM THE LORD TO A TROUBLED SOUL CAN CHANGE EVERYTHING IN A INSTANT.**

The gifts operating in the Body of Christ should be what happens normally, and not an exception to the rule. These gifts were given to the Body of Christ so that God can use us in the supernatural, like Jesus was used, and even greater.

> *Verily, verily I say unto you, He that believeth on me, the works that I do shall he do also; and greater works than these shall he do; because I go unto my Father.*
> John 14:12, KJV

The gift of the word of knowledge reveals to us things about a person that will let them know God knows them, understands, and He cares enough to reveal something about them to His servants. I have seen the word of knowledge open the hearts of the coldest and most indifferent people. It's like something breaks, faith arises, and God visits them.

I have also been given prophetic words that brought hope to the hopeless in a instant. These encounters reveal truth, the truth of what God says about a person. And this truth can set the captive free.

COMPASSION

> *And Jesus went forth, and saw a great multitude, and was moved with compassion toward them, and he healed their sick.* Matthew 14:14, KJV

When Jesus saw the multitude, He was moved with compassion (empathy) for them. He felt what they were going through. Every time the Word says that Jesus was moved with compassion in this way, miracles followed. Through this experience, we have learned that when we take time to listen to people around us, and then listen to what the Holy Spirit says, it changes us.

THROUGH THIS EXPERIENCE, WE HAVE LEARNED THAT WHEN WE TAKE TIME TO LISTEN TO PEOPLE AROUND US, AND THEN LISTEN TO WHAT THE HOLY SPIRIT SAYS, IT CHANGES US.

We are able to feel what they feel, and God honors our compassion for them and shows up to demonstrate His love.

The Lord showed me that this is what the last-days Church will operate in to bring God's presence on the earth. It's not enough just to hand out food, say a prayer, or give out a bottle of water. We, as the representatives of Christ, must engage with people, take time to listen to them, hear what the Spirit is saying about them and demonstrate God's love for them through compassion. This is what will unlock miracles, signs, wonders, and healing to flow through the Body of Christ in these last days.

What is so amazing about this is that every believer can flow in this heart of compassion.

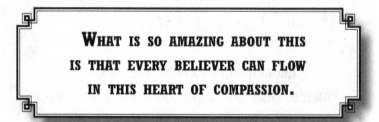

WHAT IS SO AMAZING ABOUT THIS IS THAT EVERY BELIEVER CAN FLOW IN THIS HEART OF COMPASSION.

God has not reserved His authority for miracles and healing for a few recognized men and women of God only. He will flow through children, through teens or through those who have sat on the church pew for years. God is no respecter of persons. Jesus is looking for those that will feel what other people feel and simply believe God will do a work through the life of those that touch the heart of God with compassion for the hurting. Will you be one of those?

CHAPTER 7

IN CONCLUSION

To go through the pain and discomfort during the most horrific spiritual battle of our lives was the most difficult thing we ever experienced. But knowing how much God loves us, and those that are blinded by the reality of living in a sin-sick world has transformed our thinking about our mission in these last days.

We can see that the only hope for this world is a spiritual awakening. There must be a world-wide revival of the Church of Jesus Christ. His Church will be a powerful, united force to awaken the masses of those who are lost and in despair, being held captive by the enemy.

We are so privileged to live in these times of great darkness. For when there is great darkness, the light can shine so much brighter. But first, we must be the Church that shines. It is Jesus' Church that is called to be ambassadors to this world, the representatives of a Kingdom that wants none to perish, but all to come to repentance.

How can this happen unless the Body of Christ becomes the voice of truth and compassion to all those they come into contact with. We have a mission, and it's called the Great Commission:

> **WE HAVE A MISSION, AND IT'S CALLED THE GREAT COMMISSION!**

And he said unto them, Go ye into all the world, and preach the gospel to every creature. He that believeth and is baptized shall be saved; but he that believeth not shall be damned. And these signs shall follow them that believe; In my name shall they cast out devils; they shall speak with new tongues; They shall take up serpents; and if they drink

any deadly thing, it shall not hurt them;
they shall lay hands on the sick, and they
shall recover.   Mark 16:15-18, KJV

It is not an option to be contemplated and decided whether we will do it or not. Every believer has been commissioned by God Almighty. It is important that we find our place in this ministry. People are waiting for you to care about them and have compassion for them. Jesus is waiting for you to ask what your part will be.

What can you do? It's very simple:

- Find a person in desperation. Then listen to them. Care about what they care about.
- Feel what they feel.
- Give them God's truth to the lies that keep them bond.
- Be compassionate and touch Heaven for them. Then watch what God will do.

As you individually do this, then connect with others who are also doing it:

- Expand your thinking by uniting with others who are showing compassion for the destitute.
- Pray together.
- Keep your mission focused on the lost and hurting.
- Train others to do what you are doing. Even if it is just one person, that effectively multiplies your efforts.

We don't have much time, so don't waste a minute. One day Jesus will be coming to take us home. How many people will you be taking with you? For that is the only thing we can take to heaven with us.

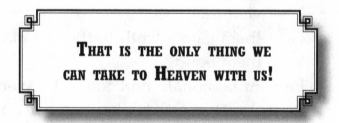

THAT IS THE ONLY THING WE CAN TAKE TO HEAVEN WITH US!

Author Contact
Information

Billy Webre
214 Julies Street
Gray, LA 70359-4922

Phone 985-991-0079
Email: bwebre42@yahoo.com

Facebook pages:
Billy Webre or
Back from the Brink (group)

REACH Ministries

We are currently connecting to five-fold ministry leaders in the Body of Christ all over the U.S. in an effort to unite the Church in these last days. We are working to raise up an army of soul-winners, filled with power, demonstrating God's love to a world desperately in need of a Savior.

Please contact us if you would like for us to come to your area or church for outreach training, ministry activation, revival services or to share our testimony.

CPSIA information can be obtained
at www.ICGtesting.com
Printed in the USA
BVHW080003211221
624507BV00006B/188